ONE MINUTE TENNIS
SERVICE SOLUTION

Stephen James Bourne

One minute tennis service solution

Copyright © 2023 by Stephen James Bourne. All rights reserved under International Copyright law. Permission is given to copy extracts from this book for personal study or sharing with friends on a non-profit basis. Or else, no part of this publication may be reproduced, stored in a retrieval system or transmitted in any form or by any means, mechanical, electronic, photocopies or otherwise without the prior written consent of the copyright owner. Any unauthorized copying, broadcasting, public performance or re-recording will constitute an infringement of copyright. Registration of this copyright is held with the International Copyright Service.

Printed in Amazon Paperback
Website: www.amazon.com

Printed in United States of America

Stephen James Bourne
YouTube: @oneminutetennis

First Printing, February 2023

ISBN: 9798378681938

CONTENTS

THE ONE MINUTE SYSTEM 4

HOW TO USE THIS GUIDE 6

SERVICE LEG DRIVE BIOMECHANICS 11

SERVICE LEG DRIVE SOLUTION 13

BIOMECHANICS OF THE BALL TOSS 16

BALL TOSS SOLUTION 18

BIOMECHANICS OF THE ARM ACTION 23

SERVICE ARM ACTION SOLUTION 26

BIOMECHANICS OF THE WRIST 34

SERVICE WRIST SOLUTION 39

FEEL GOOD OR FUNNY STORIES 43

ABOUT THE AUTHOR 45

The One Minute System

"Hi, I'm Steve, welcome to my One Minute Tennis System."

For many years I was privileged to run a very successful tennis academy. I worked with high-level players, world-class juniors and recreational players of all ages and levels.

During this time I studied anatomy and biomechanics and developed a deep understanding of the scientific principles of tennis.

Utilizing my knowledge of the science and physics of the game I created a unique teaching system based on feel, sensation, and imagery.
This system proved to be incredibly successful with players of all levels.

The Language of the Mind is Words
The Language of the Body is Feeling!

The One Minute System is based on a simple principle.
Essential teaching - the moment where the player understands and learns a new movement is much more effective if it occurs in One Minute or less!

Traditional teaching methods label us as either a

Visual Learner
Audible Learner
Kinesthetic Learner

This is often called VAK teaching and is how tennis has been taught throughout history.
People often say

"I have to see this written down"

"I have to see things" or

"I have to feel this"

Of course, they are all right, seeing, feeling, and touching are essential for learning practical skills.
But I created a better way, helping players to learn incredibly quickly, in an almost superhuman fashion. To achieve this we communicate to all of the learning senses at the same time.

This is called *Blended Learning or Blended Teaching.*

1. Feel the movement.

2. See the movement.

3. Understand the movement.

How to Use this Guide

Improving your tennis game is normally difficult and time-consuming. It does not have to be like that.

There is a better way, the ONE-MINUTE TENNIS way.

This book provides you with a combination of detailed biomechanical movements and instant tennis coaching solutions.

In precise detail, I will explain the exact movements that the best players in the world consistently use.

The techniques that I refer to are not unique to any single player. **Every movement I describe is used by all of the top 100 male and female players in the world.**

Simply understanding tennis techniques is not going to result in an improvement in your game.
It will not result in great play and often will simply be confusing.

To help you really improve your tennis this book provides incredibly effective One Minute Solutions.

Solutions that are so easy to apply and so easy to remember that they are almost impossible to forget.

This is a unique blend of science and teaching!

Science helps you to understand the stroke.

One Minute Solutions helps you improve your stroke.

These solutions work almost instantly.
To benefit from them, take your time to really "feel" and visualize the strokes, movements and changes.
At first use shadow strokes and slow controlled practice and quickly you will see your real tennis potential emerge.

As well as using One Minute Solutions you can also study the precise science and biomechanics of each aspect of the strokes to understand how the modern tennis game really works.

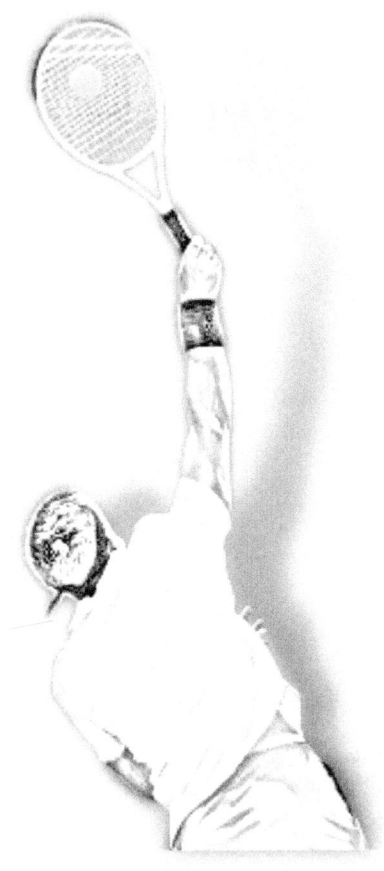

Visualize, Feel & Understand Tennis

For example when you visit your Physician.

A bad physician will bewilder you. He will probably give you long and detailed explanations that demonstrate his command of medical terminology using words that few of us can understand.

Leaving you with suggestions that are impossible to implement and therefore, essentially a highly educated waste of your time.

This is exhausting and confusing.

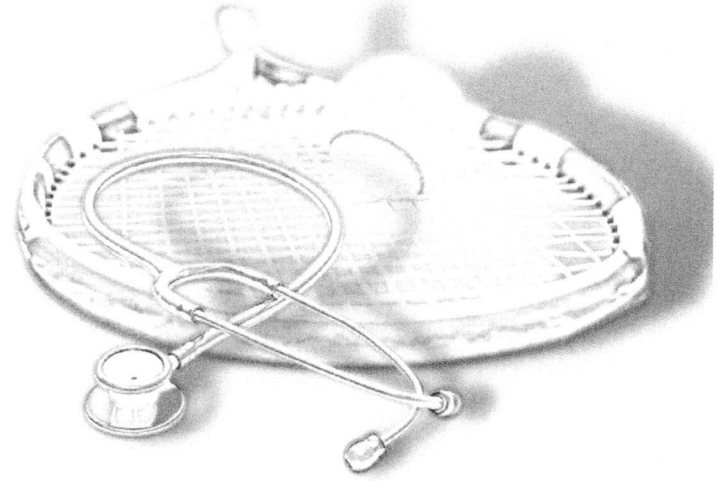

An average physician will give you a pill and send you away. He may be right, but can you trust him?
How do you know that his advice is well-informed and relevant?

A great physician will explain the science of your condition and provide possible solutions and remedies.

Then, they will give you a simple and easy-to-follow treatment or better still a magic pill that just works.

This physician can be trusted. Following his advice and suggestions is natural, beneficial, and easy.

Using the same method as the great physician.

I will show you the science, anatomy, and biomechanics of each aspect of the service and then provide a simple easy-to-follow way of recreating the movements of the world's greatest players.

I will give you the "magic pill"

To make the book easy to use I will break down the service into Four areas;

1. The lower body, knee bend, and leg drive.

2. The ball toss and how to control the placement of the bal.

3. The arm movement and kinetic chain.

4. The wrist movement and how to use it for maximum acceleration.

At the end of each One Minute Solution, I provide a link to the same lesson in video format.

Service Leg Drive Biomechanics

The biomechanics of the service from the ground to the waist are complex and necessitate the coordination and activation of numerous muscles, bones, and joints.

Preparation of your lower body With your feet shoulder-width apart and your weight equally distributed, you should begin in a balanced stance.
Your service now has a solid foundation.

1. Loading Phase:
During the loading phase, your knee bends, resulting in lower body torque and a build up of potential energy.
A slight forward lean of your trunk and a slight elevation of your racket are also part of this phase.

2. Phase of push-off:
You transfer the energy generated during the loading phase to your upper body by pushing off your front foot and extending your front leg.
Then shift your weight from your back foot to your front foot during this phase.

3. Activation of muscle:
Your quadriceps, hamstrings, and calf muscles are involved in your service's leg drive. These muscles work together to generate power and speed. During your service, your hip and trunk are also stabilized by the gluteal muscles.

Biomechanics

4. Extending the knee:
Fully extend your front knee, transferring energy to your upper body from the ground up.

5. Extending the hip:
Your hip must extend, transferring more power from your lower body to your upper body.

6. Footwork:
During your leg drive, footwork is also crucial. To help absorb the impact of your service and avoid injury, you should aim to land on your front foot with your knee slightly bent.

Feet Anatomy:
The bones in your feet help to transfer power from the ground and provide a stable foundation for your service. The plantar flexors and dorsiflexor muscles in your feet aid in maintaining stability and balance.

Legs:
During your serve, your legs' femur, tibia, and fibula bones provide support and power. Strength and stability is generated by the muscles of your quadriceps, hamstrings, and glutes.

Spine:
During your serve, your back muscles, including the erector spinae, aid in maintaining stability and producing power.

Abdominals:
The stability and power transferred from your legs to your upper body is provided by your abs.

Service Leg Drive Solution

"Bend your knees!"
Does that sound familiar?

**It is important to understand that you do not bend your knees...
your knees just bend!**

Let me explain...

Knees are not designed to push the body upwards, they function efficiently when lowering your body. For example, sitting down.

So focusing on bending your knees to assist a powerful leg drive that requires upward force is pointless.

Consider everyday activities that require you to bend your knees.
Are you reading this sitting down?
Did you even think which knee should be bent first? Or how much your knees needed to bend?
No you simply sat down?
Standing up and sitting down is a totally natural movement.

So what do we need to focus on?

To efficiently generate power from the ground upwards.
As your hands move upwards into "Trophy Pose" more or less where your racket hand passes over your shoulder.
Push your weight forwards into your toes and raise your heels.
As a result of this your knees will bend.

SOLUTION

Remember you should not deliberately bend your knees.
Your knees bend naturally as part of the whole service movement!

When your weight is pushed forward and your heels are raised, your feet, ankles, and calves are fully engaged and ready to violently push your body upwards. This position is ideal for transferring momentum and energy through the knees into the body, arm, racket and ball!

Your service will be easier, faster, and more natural.
Your entire body will automatically drive upwards as a result of your leg drive coming from the ground, beginning from your feet and NOT your knees.

Tennis strokes are more effective when we don't overthink the technique.
All other movements will automatically occur by raising your heels at the right moment

For a smooth, powerful, easy serve Don't bend your knees. Your knees bend.

SOLUTION

Heels Up
weight
loaded forwards
ready for strong
leg drive

Heels Down
knees bent
ready for weak
leg drive

YouTube Lesson
https://youtu.be/Qg9Jb8C2jHU

Biomechanics of the ball toss

The ball toss in tennis is a crucial part of your service, and involves a combination of upper and lower extremities, your torso, and eye-hand coordination.

Correct balance and stability are necessary for a successful ball toss. This starts from your feet.

Your legs provide the foundation for the rest of your body to move efficiently.

Your torso is the central part of your body and plays a crucial role in generating power for your ball toss.

The rotational movement of your torso involves the activation of your oblique and rectus abdominis muscles, which provide the necessary force to generate a high-velocity serve

Biomechanics

Your shoulder girdle and arm are also involved in the ball toss.
Your shoulder joint is a ball and socket joint that allows for a wide range of motion, including overhead motion necessary for the serve.
Your rotator cuff muscles, deltoids, and triceps brachii are important for stabilizing your shoulder and generating the force needed to propel the ball.

Your hand and wrist also play a role in the ball toss, as they are responsible for releasing the ball into the air.
Your forearm, wrist muscles and tendons provide the fine motor control for a precise ball release.

Finally, the eye-hand coordination is also important in your ball toss.
Your visual system must accurately track the ball from the release to the point of impact, and your hand must respond accordingly to make the necessary adjustments for a successful serve.

In conclusion, the ball toss in tennis requires the coordination of multiple body systems, including the legs, torso, shoulder girdle, arm, hand, wrist, and visual system.

Ball Toss Solution

The ball toss!
Surely the simplest part of your service, you just put the ball into the right place and hit it?

This is true unless you are in the 99% of players who find the ball toss the most frustrating, annoying, and damaging part of their serve.

For most players, the problems with their ball toss stem from one of, or a combination of two technical issues.
These are;
The release of the ball from the hand.
Or the arm movement itself, as the ball, is launched upwards.

Let's start by looking at the movement of your hand

SOLUTION

The ball flying inconsistently out of control from your hand is almost always a result of the ball spinning as it leaves your fingers.
Therefore removing that spin is essential.

To correct this and make a simple ball toss with zero or almost zero spin we need to look at a sport where spinning the ball is controlled and understood. In cricket, the ability of the bowler to spin the ball is essential.
To achieve this spin, the bowler uses 'spinning fingers' These are the two middle fingers.

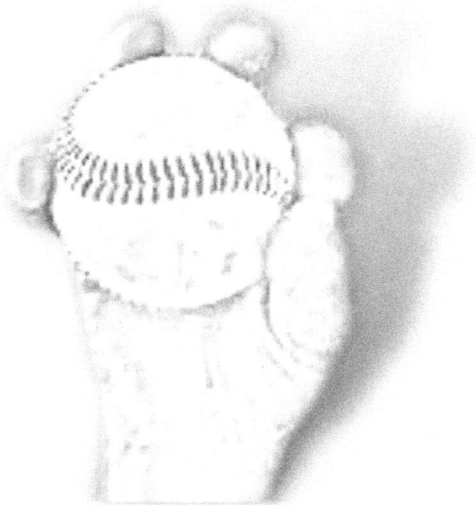

It is probably more precise to think of these as the "spinning fingertips" because the finger tips are the significant factor in spinning the ball.

If the ball makes contact with the spinning fingertips then it is almost impossible not to spin it significantly.
If the spinning fingertips do not make contact the ball then it is almost impossible to spin the ball.

SOLUTION

So, we have to look at how to remove the spin and bring the ball under control as it is released from your hand.

A great way of doing this is to put tape on your spinning fingertips. With this tape in place, you will be able to feel any contact between your fingertips and the ball.

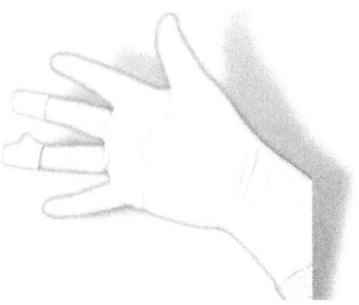

As you release the ball it is important to spread your fingers, keeping the largest distance possible between the ball and your spinning fingers.

Very quickly you will start to see the ball leaving your hand with zero, or almost zero rotation.

The ball will now be under control and travel in a straight and precise direction.

You can practice this movement with your eyes closed, to 'feel' the correct release of the ball.
It will not take long to apply this simple solution and the benefit to the control of your ball toss will be instant and significant

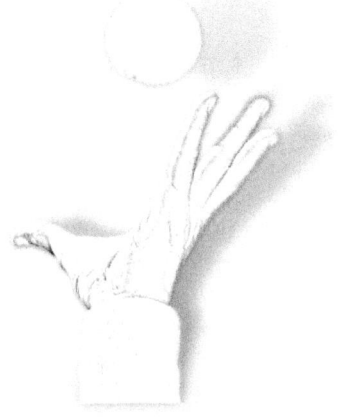

SOLUTION

The other significant cause of an out-of-controlled ball toss is the shape and rhythm of your arm.

This can be because the elbow bends in the middle of the action, creating a flicking movement, or because your arm shoots up way too quickly losing all control of the ball.

A great solution for this is to imagine that you have a piece of elastic looped around your left wrist and left foot.
Now imagine that as you make the ball toss and raise your hand, you are stretching the imaginary elastic.

SOLUTION

This means that instead of just elevating your arm, you are stretching and separating your hand and foot.
Your ball toss will now be made with your whole body and not just your arm.

By using this image of the imaginary elastic, the feeling and rhythm of your ball toss will be transformed.
With little practice, your ball toss will become precise and controlled.

These two solutions are simple, easy to apply, require little practice, and will work almost instantly.
Transforming your ball toss in minutes.

YouTube Lesson
https://youtu.be/t26oZbOn3to

Biomechanics of the Arm Action

The biomechanics and anatomy of the service arm movement in tennis, involves the complex coordination of various joints, muscles, and bones in your arm, shoulder, and back. Here's a breakdown of how your service arm movement works:

Shoulder rotation:

The main power for your service comes from the rotational movement of your shoulder joint. Your rotator cuff muscles, including the supraspinatus, infraspinatus, teres minor and subscapularis. These are crucial for stabilizing your shoulder and allowing for smooth and powerful rotation.

Biomechanics

Scapular movement:

Your scapula, or shoulder blade, also plays a crucial role in your service stroke. The scapula helps to provide stability to your shoulder joint and helps to transfer the power generated by your shoulder to your arm.

The muscles that control scapular movement, such as the trapezius, serratus anterior, and rhomboids, also play an important role in your service movement.

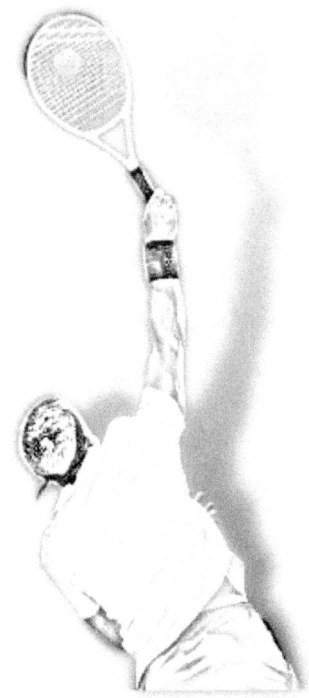

Elbow flexion and extension:

Your elbow joint plays major a role in your service movement, with your biceps and triceps muscles controlling elbow flexion and extension, respectively.

During your service motion, the elbow starts in a flexed position and then rapidly extends to generate speed and power.

Biomechanics

Wrist and hand movements:

Your wrist and hand also play a role in your service movement, with the wrist pronating and supinating to generate spin on the ball. Your hand muscles, including the forearm flexors and extensors, work together to control the speed and trajectory of the ball.

It's important to note that the service arm movement in tennis is a highly repetitive motion that can put significant stress on the arm and shoulder.

Overuse injuries, such as rotator cuff strains, tennis elbow, and shoulder impingement, without correct technique, are common among tennis players.

Service Arm Action Solution

The correct arm action is the most important aspect of developing a consistent, effortless, and powerful service.

To achieve real power, it is essential that your arm is segmented through the stroke.
The upper arm, forearm, hand and racket must be traveling in different directions, and yet aligning for a fraction of a second at the exact moment of contact with the ball.

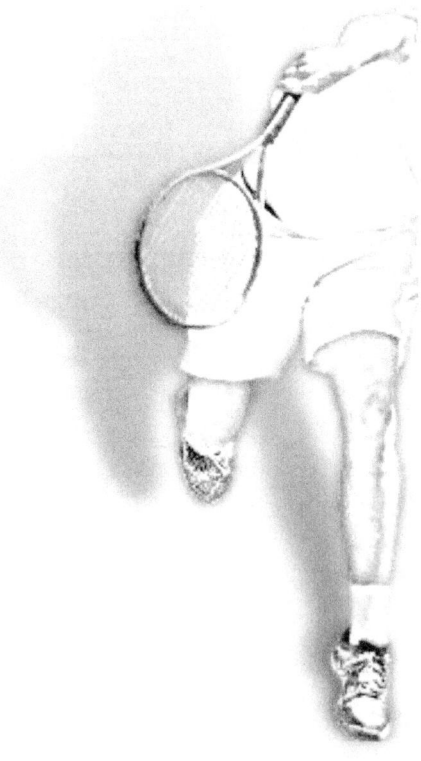

Solution

This combination of an unnatural movement and precise timing makes the service stroke one of the most difficult movements in sport.

Because of the complexities of this, we have to learn the stroke with "feel" and not by breaking the stroke down into individual pieces.

To feel the correct arm action, begin with no racket, just your arm! Make your arm as loose as possible.

Solution

Feel that your wrist is loose and floppy and that your arm has zero stress.
Now go through the service movement and as your arm passes your head, hit your right elbow with your left hand and stop the forward movement of your elbow.

As a result of this, your arm should fly away from your body. This action has created a kinetic chain. Remember kinetic chains always work from the ground up and from the inside of the body in an outwards direction.

Solution

The left hand catches your elbow.

As a result your hand and forearm accelerate forwards.

Solution

After a few repetitions, repeat the same process, but this time whilst holding the racket.

This is actually easier than without the racket as the weight and momentum of your racket will assist the acceleration and momentum of the swing when your left hand stops your elbow.

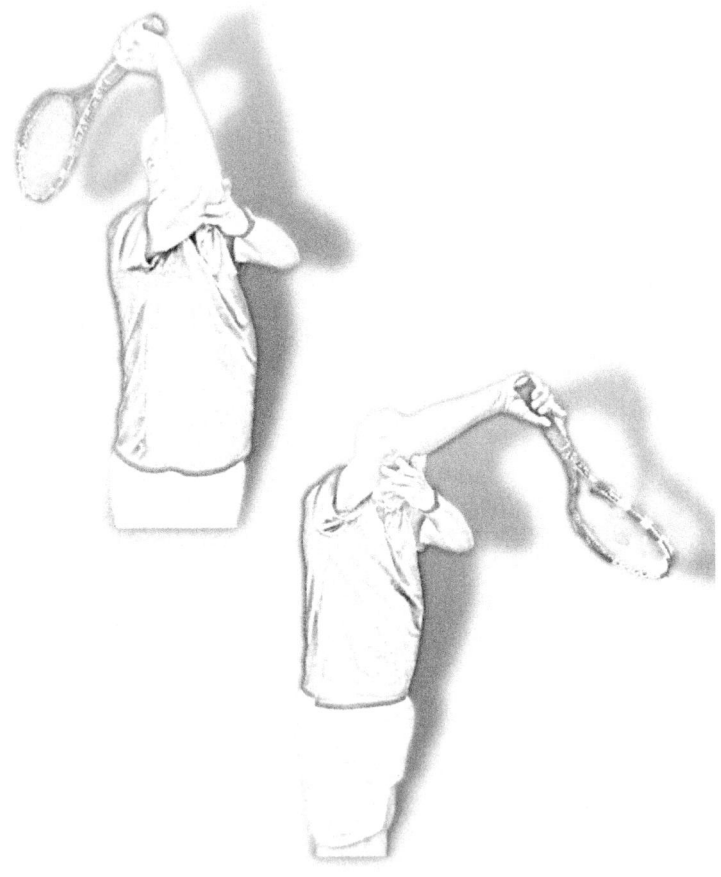

Solution

After more repetitions, the next progression is to alternate between shadow-swinging the racket while still using your left hand to stop your elbow.
Then repeat the movement without using your left hand but be sure to that your elbow slows or stops.

You now should be experiencing the feeling of your elbow stopping.
This is the elbow snap.
Many traditional coaches talk about the wrist snap.

In reality, the wrist snap is a by-product of the elbow snap.

Solution

**Now let's add the tennis ball and make a full service stroke.
Be sure to repeat the same movement with your elbow slowing or stopping. The "feeling" of your service should be totally different. Less effort but more power.**

You should now be enjoying the easy power that the perfect arm action delivers.

Solution

If you lose power or feel that your service has become hard work requiring great effort.

Simply repeat the shadow stroke using your left hand to hold your elbow back. Once again you will immediately feel the acceleration of your forearm, hand, and racket as it speeds past your upper arm.

Because you have now simply reminded yourself of the correct movement, it will be simple to re-apply it to your service stroke

With this simple and easy-to-apply movement, your service will be energized and effortless.

YouTube Lesson
https://youtu.be/LdsE6YSgRm4

Biomechanics of the Wrist

The wrist action of your service is an important aspect of the biomechanics of your stroke, greatly affecting the power and accuracy of your serve.

During your service motion, your wrist plays a key role in generating racket head speed and control.

At the beginning of the service, your wrist should be in a neutral and relaxed position.

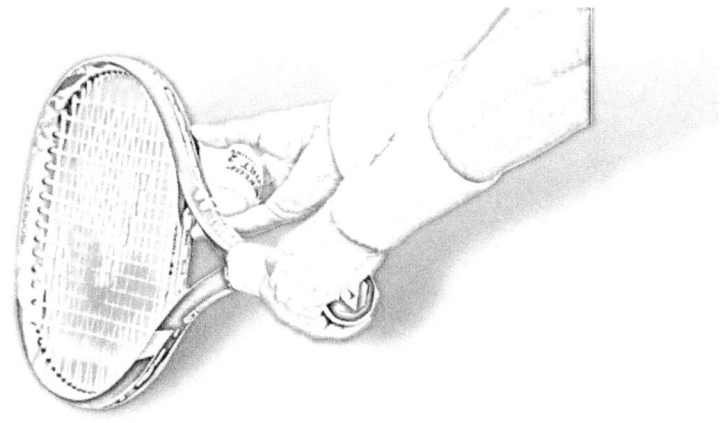

As you initiate the forward swing, your wrist should begin to extend with flexion. Resulting on your racket head accelerating through the contact point with the ball.

Biomechanics

Your wrist action during the follow-through phase of the service is important.

After you have hit the ball your wrist should continue to extend. This extension will have ensured that your racket head was accelerating through contact with the ball.
Generating maximum power and spin.

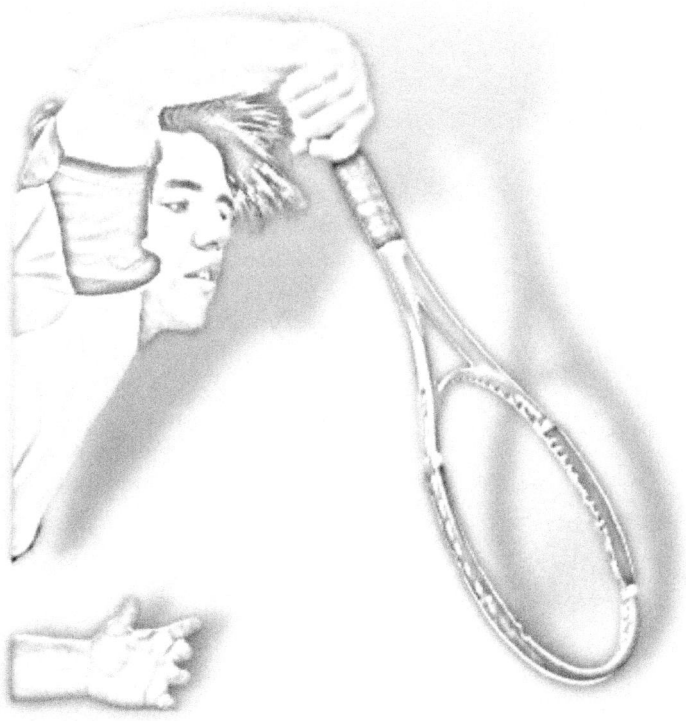

It's important to note that your wrist action during the tennis serve should be a fluid and natural motion, not forced or tense. It is useful to work on strengthening your wrist and forearm muscles through exercises such as wrist curls, wrist extensions, and grip strengthening exercises.

Biomechanics

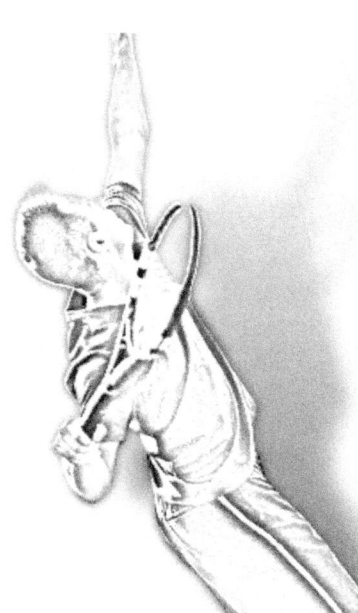

Loading phase:
During the loading phase of the serve, your wrist is in a neutral position, meaning that it is not flexed or extended. At this stage you should grip your racket loosely allowing your wrist to naturally bend backwards as your racket moves into the trophy position.
Your wrist extensors, which are a group of muscles on the back of your forearm, are activated during this phase to keep your wrist in a neutral position.

Extension phase:
As you begin to draw your racket forward, the wrist starts to be loaded using extension, which means that it is being stretched or bent forwards. This motion is initiated by the wrist flexors, which are a group of muscles on the front of your forearm. Your wrist should be cocked to an angle of approximately 90 degrees at the point where your racket is about to drop into the swing.

Biomechanics

Acceleration phase:
As your racket starts to drop into the swing, your wrist begins to uncock or extend. This motion is initiated by the wrist extensors and can generate a significant amount of racket head speed. Your wrist extension should continue until the point of maximum extension, which should occur just after the ball has been struck.

Follow-through phase:
After hitting the ball , your wrist should continue to extend, allowing your racket head to speed through contact with the ball and your arm to fully stretch.
This motion is important for generating maximum power and spin on your serve.
Your wrist extensors are activated again during this phase to maintain your wrist in an extended position.

Biomechanics

Anatomically, the wrist joint is composed of eight small bones called the carpal bones, which are connected to the bones of the forearm, the radius and ulna, and the many small bones of your hand.

The wrist is stabilized by several ligaments and tendons, which are attached to the bones and muscles in your forearm.

Your wrist flexors are primarily composed of the flexor carpi radialis, the flexor carpi ulnaris, and the palmaris longus muscles. Your wrist extensors are primarily composed of the extensor carpi radialis, the extensor carpi ulnaris, and the extensor digitorum muscles.

In summary, your wrist action in your service involves a complex interplay between your wrist flexors and extensors, and is important for generating racket head speed and control.

Service Wrist Solution

Correct wrist movement is a vital aspect of developing a smooth, effortless, and powerful service.

It is essential that the racket is accelerating through contact with the ball.

For the very fortunate players who have a 'natural' throwing action this wrist movement seems very simple.
However, for the majority of players who do not have a 'natural' throwing action, the wrist movement is a substantial reason that their service is weaker and slower than it should be.

The problem is that the huge range of motion of the wrist required for a great service occurs in a fraction of a second and in a very small part of the stroke. This is often called the wrist "snap" and should happen exactly through contact with the ball. This combination of complex movements in a short space of time make it even more difficult to consciously adjust the technique.

Our One Minute Solution for this is simple and easy.

Begin by holding your racket in a 'choked up' grip, above the handle of your racket and the throat of your racket.

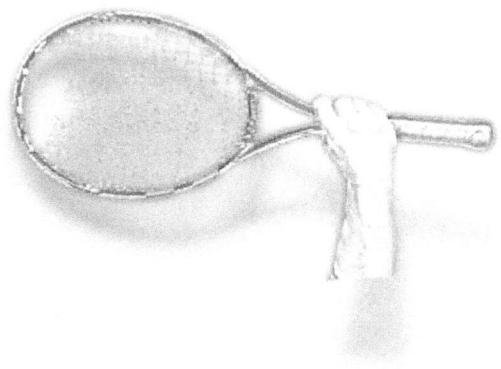

Solution

Now make a shadow stroke without the ball and stop with your racket in front of your body.

Your racket handle should now have passed your hand and be pointing away from your body.

If your racket handle is behind your hand and pointing into your body then your wrist is slowing your service down.

If your racket handle is level with your arm and pointing slightly away from your body then your wrist is neither slowing nor accelerating your service.

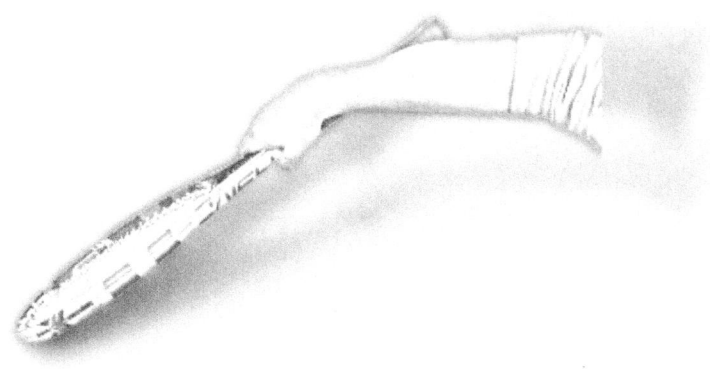

Solution

If your racket handle is past your hand and pointing distinctly away from your body then your wrist is "helping" the acceleration of your service stroke.

Still using the 'choked-up grip' now progress to hitting the ball. It will feel very inhibited but even with this grip your serve should be a little faster.

Now alternate between serving with the choked-up grip and serving with your normal grip. *It is important that when you use your normal grip you check that you are finishing in your new ending and not immediately reverting back to your old habits.*

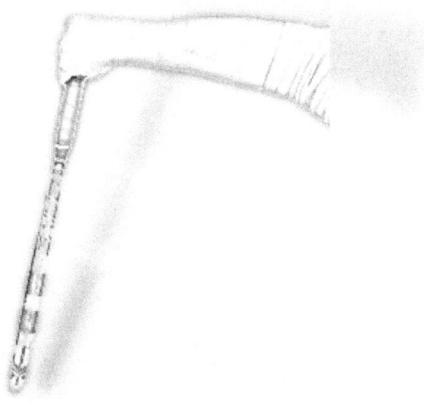

Solution

This use of the 'choked-up grip' is a great way of finding the correct wrist movement and adding power to your serve.

Once you have felt "the correct movement" your old stroke will feel strange and slow and your new swing will become natural and easy to reproduce.

YouTube Lesson
https://www.youtube.com/watch?v=QBUzA3tHNO8

FEEL GOOD OR FUNNY STORIES

Over a lifetime of teaching tennis at every possible level, I have met some amazing people and seen many amusing things.

In each of my One Minute Tennis Books, I will share a true story that I found amusing or fascinating.

A few years ago I coached a wonderful young player called Sebastian.

When he was just 8 years old I entered him for only his second tournament in the 10 and under age group.

Sebastian made it to the semi-finals of the tournament, which was an amazing result.

The story I want to share occurred in his quarter-final match

Solution

Playing very well, in the quarter-finals Seb had a great match...

The match was just one set.

At 4-5 30-40, Seb had a match point.

The other boy had to serve.
His first serve was in the net. He then hit a terrible, slow floating second serve that was at least a foot out.
Seb's father shouted "yes" as the match was won with this huge double fault.

Seb said nothing, no call of "out." Nothing!
They played a long tense rally, the other boy won the rally.

The match continued and after several tense minutes, Sebastian eventually won the match for a second time.

We were all pleased for him.. but later, in a quiet moment I asked him "Why didn't you call that ball out... The second service on march point, it was way out?"

He looked at me like I was crazy then replied

"I just want to play, if I called 'out' the match was over, I wanted to keep playing tennis!"

I hope we all keep some of that innocent love of this truly wonderful game..

STEPHEN JAMES BOURNE

I have been involved in tennis all of my life. As a player I was a good hitter, I was ranked in the top 30 players in the UK, often helping professional players prepare for matches.

Having previously coached in the USA, Arabia and the UK I ran my own tennis academy for many years on the Eastern coast of Spain. For over 20 years we worked with every imaginable type of player. Beginner to professional, young and old (my oldest client was 93 years of age)

Aided by a large team of coaches I developed a unique approach to teaching (see The One Minute System on page 3) This system proved to be amazingly successful at all levels. During this time both recreational and competitive players requested online help and written information on the teaching methods that they had experienced and benefitted from. The pandemic gave me the opportunity to take this teaching philosophy online and the One Minute Tennis YouTube channel began. The channel enjoyed amazing success with over 2,000,000 views in the first year.
https://www.youtube.com/channel/UCbmBx0-ZS9V7KSbyhrZcYqw

The purpose of this series of Tennis Solutions Books is to help recreational and developing players use the techniques of the best players in the world.

The combination of the scientific principles of the latest techniques in tennis along with my quick and easy-to-follow One Minute Solutions make a complicated game simple and will help you to play better tennis today!

YOUR NEXT ONE MINUTE TENNIS BOOK WILL BE OUT SOON

Printed in Great Britain
by Amazon